Swimming with Hammerhead Sharks

BY KENNETH MALLORY

A New England Aquarium Book

Houghton Mifflin Company
Boston 2001

To the scientists who help bring their unique perspective and understanding
to children and their families around the world

Photo Credits
Pages 1, 4, 8 (right), 10, 15, 17, 18, 20, 23, 28 (bottom), 36, 41, 42 (top), 43, 44, and front cover: Howard Hall/HHP
Pages 6 (top), 11, 25, 26, 30, 31, 32, 33 (bottom), 34 (top), 38, 39, 45, 46, and back cover: Michele Hall/HHP
Pages 3, 47: John Dunham
Pages 5, 8 (left), 19: Paul Erickson, New England Aquarium
Page 6: IMAX Corporation
Pages 7, 12, 14, 16 (top), 21: Don Nelson
Page 16 (bottom): Pete Klimley
Pages 28, 29, 33 (top), 35: Kenneth Mallory, New England Aquarium
Pages 37, 42 (bottom): Mark Conlin

www.houghtonmifflinbooks.com

The text of this book is set in Poppl-Laudatio.
Map and illustrations by Jerry Malone

Library of Congress Cataloging-in-Publication Data

Mallory, Kenneth.
Swimming with hammerhead sharks / Kenneth Mallory, in association with the New England Aquarium.
p. cm.
Includes bibliographical references (p.).
ISBN 0-618-05543-6
1. Hammerhead sharks — Research — Juvenile literature. [1. Hammerhead sharks.
2. Sharks.] I. New England Aquarium (Boston, Mass.) II. Title.
QL638.95.S7 M36   2000
597.3'4 — dc21   00-061401

Printed in Hong Kong
SCP 10 9 8 7 6 5 4 3 2 1

Acknowledgments

I wish to thank New England Aquarium President Jerry R. Schubel for opening my window on Cocos Island and for creating his vision of the New England Aquarium as a public aquatic academy; Pete Klimley for sharing his shark dreams and adventures; Howard and Michele Hall for introducing me to their underwater artistry; and WGBH, as represented by NOVA Executive Producer Paula Apsell, Executive Producer of Large Format Films Suzanne Simpson, Science Adviser/Writer Joe Levine, Kelly Tyler, Lisa Roberts, and Peter Tyson. I am especially indebted to the many scientists I have met in my career who have taught me to value, respect, and preserve life on land and in the sea.

I explore the waters of Cocos Island.

Shark Scientist

I met my first shark in about twenty feet of water near Midnight Pass, off Siesta Key, in Sarasota, Florida. It was small—two feet long at most—a juvenile nurse shark that was hiding under coral rock ledges a few hundred feet out from the beach. As I floated at the surface preparing to dive for a closer look, I rehearsed Genie's instructions. "You have to sneak up on them," she had said, "and grab them by the gills."

Genie was Eugenie Clark, then director of the Cape Haze Marine Laboratory, author of *Lady with a Spear* and *The Lady and the Sharks,* and my teacher while I was a volunteer in the summer of 1969. She had set up a shark pen near the marine lab to run some of the first experiments on shark eyesight. The "baby" nurse sharks Genie asked me to catch were to be part of that shark-pen experiment.

I didn't capture any nurse sharks that day—someone else did—but the summer at Cape Haze (now Mote Marine Laboratory) changed the way I looked at sharks forever. Scientists were just beginning to make revolutionary adjustments in our understanding of how sharks live and what role they play in the ocean ecosystem.

As we begin the twenty-first century, sharks are in trouble. Overfishing, accidental capture in fishing nets (called "bycatch"), the fatal practice of removing sharks'

The New England Aquarium's Giant Ocean Tank contains nurse sharks like this one because they are relatively docile and adjust well to this exhibit.

Above: Shark fins are stripped from hammerheads and other sharks for shark-fin soup and other Asian delicacies.

Below: The IMAX movie poster.

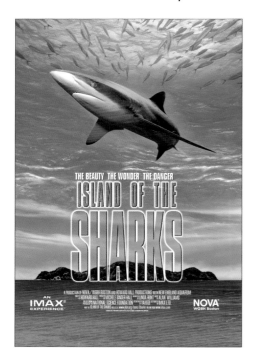

fins for shark-fin soup, and the senseless killing of sharks just because they are sharks are all taking their toll on shark populations around the world. Those of us who care about what is happening feel an increasing urgency to get to the truth about sharks and to educate others.

You can imagine my excitement when, thirty years after seeing my first shark in Florida waters, the New England Aquarium sent me on a mission that would bring me face to face with hundreds of scalloped hammerhead sharks. The goal of the mission was to tell the story of these incredible animals.

To provide the opening film for a planned new IMAX theater, the New England Aquarium teamed with the science documentary film group NOVA, part of WGBH TV, to create a movie called *Island of the Sharks.* IMAX films are what filmmakers call large-format films—they are projected on screens 4,500 times bigger than a mid-size TV screen (they are the height of a two-story building). The IMAX shark movie would be filmed in the waters surrounding a small island off the Pacific coast of Costa Rica, Central America. I would travel to Cocos Island with the filmmakers to write about my experience.

Before my trip, I needed to learn more about the sharks themselves. I sought out Pete Klimley, a marine biologist who works at the Bodega Bay Marine Lab in Bodega Bay, California. An expert on hammerhead sharks, Pete was one of the film's most important advisers.

I met Pete Klimley on the New England Aquarium plaza in Boston early one autumn morning in 1998. He is a tall man with tousled blond hair and a full mustache. He walks with the physical assurance of a former college swimmer, training he puts to good use when studying the behavior of sharks. Pete was visiting the aquarium to help shape the story of the IMAX film.

I quickly learned that Pete's approach to science and the study of animal behavior is uniquely his own. Pete told me he once squeezed his six-foot-one-inch body into a scuba diving suit painted black and white with a fin on the back to resemble a killer whale. Killer whales (also known as orcas) are among the few animals that are big and powerful enough to scare even a shark. By swimming toward a lemon shark in his killer whale disguise, Pete hoped to show that the shark would display its fear by swimming rapidly in tight circles with its mouth open wide. He got the response he expected and lived to tell about it.

I knew about sand tiger sharks, lemon sharks, and nurse sharks because they were residents of our Giant Ocean Tank exhibit at the aquarium. Aside from their oddly shaped heads, the most I could remember about hammerhead sharks was the fear they inspired in the characters in a novel by Ernest Hemingway called *Islands in the Stream.*

Pete told me that there are nine different kinds of hammerhead sharks, not just the great hammerhead *(Sphyrna mokarran),* which Hemingway had described. There are the three-foot-long scalloped bonnethead—the smallest species— the whitefin, smalleye, smooth, scoophead, winghead, bonnethead, and the species that

Pete Klimley in the 1970s, as he prepares to dive among hammerhead sharks near the Espiritu Santo seamount.

Above: Like nurse sharks, sand tiger sharks adjust well to the artificial coral reef in the New England Aquarium's Giant Ocean Tank.

Right: Schooling hammerhead sharks.

Pete is most familiar with, the scalloped hammerhead *(Sphyrna lewini)*, named for the scalloped appearance of its head when viewed from above.

What really caught my attention in Pete's description of hammerhead sharks, however, was how different they are from other kinds of sharks. Hammerheads are, evolutionarily speaking, among the newest kids on the block. They appeared about 25 million years ago, almost 400 million years after their most ancient ancestors. Their brains are among the biggest in the shark world, and they are far more sociable than most of their more solitary cousins.

Sharks get a lot of bad publicity that they don't always deserve, but sometimes they do. If you decide to go swimming off a seal haul-out area on the northern California coast,

Common name	Scientific name	Information
Bonnethead	*Sphyrna tiburo*	Found in the western Atlantic and eastern Pacific. Average length is 3.3 feet (1 meter) but can reach up to 5 feet (1.5 meters).
Great hammerhead	*Sphyrna mokarran*	Found in the western and eastern North Atlantic and the Indo-West and eastern Pacific. Can reach over 11.5 feet (3.5 meters).
Scalloped bonnethead	*Sphyrna corona*	Found in inshore waters of the eastern Pacific and waters off Central and South America. Can grow to 3 feet (.9 meters).
Scalloped hammerhead	*Sphyrna lewini*	Found in the western and eastern Atlantic, Indo-West, central and eastern Pacific. Can grow to 13 feet (4 meters).
Scoophead	*Sphyrna media*	Found in tropical inshore waters of the eastern Pacific off Central and South America, and the western North Atlantic off South and Central America. Can grow to 4.9 feet (1.5 meters).
Smalleye	*Sphyrna tudes*	Found in inshore waters of the western North Atlantic off South America. Can grow to 4.9 feet (1.5 meters).
Smooth hammerhead	*Sphyrna zygaena*	Found in the western and eastern North Atlantic; western Indian Ocean, and western, central, and eastern Pacific. Can reach up to 13 feet (4 meters).
Whitefin	*Sphyrna couardi*	A coastal and pelagic (living in the open ocean) bottom dweller found in tropical waters off the west coast of Africa. Can reach 9.8 feet (3 meters).
Winghead	*Eusphyra blochii*	Found in the Indo-West. Can reach up to 5 feet (1.5 meters).

A blacktip shark rests after feeding on a school of fish corralled into a baitball during a cooperative hunt.

there's a possibility that a great white shark will mistake you for a seal, one of its favorite foods. White sharks and other so-called man-eaters are powerful, finely tuned eating machines. If you are in the wrong place at the wrong time, you could end up being a meal.

There are more than 390 kinds of sharks in the world, and most of them don't bother people. Cookie cutter sharks, which are slightly over a foot long, take bites the size of an ice cream scoop out of unsuspecting whales, tunas, and porpoises. Then there are basking sharks, forty-foot-long giants whose idea of a good meal is the plankton soup that floats in the water around them.

Sharks deserve our respect and wonder. For all their bad reputation for taking human lives, sharks may someday be better known for saving them instead. Their ability to resist disease has long interested medical researchers. They may even provide clues to a cure for AIDS.

Hammerhead sharks travel singly or in groups of several hundred.

11

Schooling with a Purpose

Pete was a graduate student at the Scripps Institution of Oceanography when he learned about hammerheads in 1978. He read the unpublished field notes of the former director of the Steinhart Aquarium, Earl Herald, which described an immense school of hammerhead sharks at an undersea mountain, called a seamount, off the island of Espiritu Santo in the Gulf of California. Undersea volcanoes create seamounts that rise thousands of feet from the ocean floor but never reach the surface. For some reason, Espiritu Santo seemed to attract hammerhead sharks in schools of more than two hundred animals.

Basing his search on Earl Herald's field notes, Pete first tried to get close to the hammerheads by "chumming": throwing bait containing fish meat and oils onto the surface of the water. When that didn't attract them, he played a recording of low-frequency sounds similar to the sounds small fish make underwater, hoping that would serve as a dinner bell for sharks swimming nearby. That, too, brought no results. Finally, after nearly a year of looking and waiting, he got a chance to swim with a school of hammerhead sharks.

"The first time I did it, the water was kind of murky," Pete told me. "I could barely see the sharks, and then suddenly I was smack in the middle of them. I was close enough to reach out and touch their skin. At that time, sharks were all thought to be man-eaters, so diving down to see them went against the grain. I don't know why people thought that sharks, most of which are

Pete swimming at the surface, looking for hammerhead sharks.

about our length, would be eating us, but that's what they thought. And there they were all around me, and they were beautiful. The sun was reflecting off their sides, and they were kind of rippling as they moved."

When Pete realized these schooling scalloped hammerheads had little interest in him as a potential meal, he began to wonder why they were swimming in a school and why they had gathered at this particular undersea mountain.

Pete believes in thorough and careful observation before designing experiments. He found that he had to eliminate one of the best tools at his disposal—the scuba tank (self-contained underwater breathing apparatus)—after his first few dives. The bubbles of exhaled air scared all the hammerheads away. The best way to observe sharks was to hold his breath and "free" dive with a video camera. He sometimes dove to seventy feet, where he would film for a minute and a half before he had to return to the surface.

Pete wanted to know more about the composition of the large school: were these sharks a mixture of males and females or all of one sex? Were they adult or juvenile sharks? Answers to these questions would help him decide if the sharks were swimming in a school for defense, hunting, or perhaps finding a mate.

Pete with the video camera that he used to document hammer-head shark behavior in his early studies in the Gulf of California.

Above: Pete uses a special apparatus to take two photos of a shark simultaneously.

Below: The photographs enabled Pete to estimate the length of the hammerhead sharks.

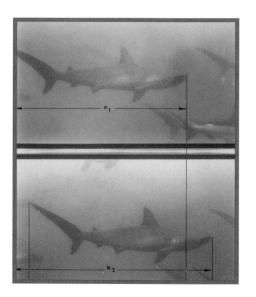

It was easy for Pete to differentiate males from females just by free-diving observation. Male sharks have a pair of visible "claspers" on their undersides near their tails, extensions of the pelvic or hip fins, which they use in mating with female sharks. But Pete needed to know more about the age of these sharks to tell if they were sexually mature. From studies of the catches made by local fishermen, he determined that males were mature when they reached a length of five and one-third feet and females when they were seven feet or more. Getting accurate measurements of the sharks in the schools was another problem altogether.

Pete invented a crossbow apparatus to measure the sharks. He attached two cameras to the crossbeam, rigging them so that both took a photo of the same shark at the same time, producing a stereoscopic image. Next Pete made measurements from the resulting photographs. Using a mathematical formula based on the distance between the cameras on the crossbeam, he was able to make a good estimate of the length of the shark.

Using free-diving observation and the crossbow apparatus, Pete discovered that nearly 80 percent of the animals in the school were females and that most of them were still too small and young to give birth. Pete could see that the school was not looking for food; he rarely saw animals chasing down a meal. Perhaps these sharks were swimming together for protection and mutual support.

But he also noticed that the biggest females fought with the other females to stake out the center of the school. They used head butts and fancy body twists to establish position. Pete called this system a "dominance hierarchy." Only the big female sharks were mature enough to mate, and among them, he observed, "the largest, physically fit females force

the smaller ones out of the center of the school, into which males dash to find a mate."
This sophisticated social behavior is evidence against the view of sharks as primitive
"killing machines."

What comes through when talking with Pete Klimley is his genuine respect and awe for
these remarkable animals. "I'm a real enemy of that whole mindset [stereotype] of sharks
and danger," he says. "The majority of sharks that you'd encounter—blue sharks, silky
sharks, pelagic whitetip sharks—are not dangerous. What happens is filmmakers go out
there and throw a lot of bait in the water, and then they see this very unusual hysteria of
sharks biting at anything. It would be the same if you threw meat to a pack of dogs that
hadn't eaten for a long period and filmed it. It's unfortunate that cinematography has
given sharks this narrow image—it's the 5 percent, not the 95 percent. I've tried in my life to fight against that mindset."

A hammerhead shark patrols the ocean waters.

Pete is working to replace the terror heightened by movies such
as *Jaws* with wonder and appreciation. "There have been times when
I wouldn't even have to dive," he observed about his experiences
with schooling hammerhead sharks. "They'd be swimming so close
to the surface that all I had to do was tread water with my feet down
and I'd be touching them. I'd be filming them and all their elaborate
behaviors—such as the reverse flip with a full twist that a female will
use as a signal to other females to move away, that she is the domi-
nant female—and they'd be looking at me. I'd be thinking, 'God,
they're intelligent. What do they think of me?'"

Magnetic Attraction

Pete had now found at least one answer to the question of why hammerhead sharks gather at seamounts in such large schools: these are social gathering places where males find females to mate with. But hundreds of hours spent observing these groups had persuaded him that seamounts served another purpose, too. Pete believes that seamounts may be centers of navigation that help sharks—and perhaps many other kinds of animals—find their way through the otherwise featureless ocean. To prove this theory, he ran an ingenious set of experiments using fish "tags" to follow sharks night and day.

Wildlife biologists have been using tags to follow land animals such as deer, lions, and birds for as long as they have been tracking animals. These tags can be as simple as a colored band around the leg of a bald eagle or as complex as a special electronic collar around the neck of a black bear that sends signals to a satellite.

Putting an effective tag on an animal that lives in water, however, has a different set of challenges. Tagging a small fish, for example, requires catching, tagging, and releasing the fish without hurting it. In following a whale, it might not be possible to maneuver close enough to make a secure attachment without a harpoon or a dart. Even if the person tagging can get close, there is no guarantee that the tag will remain in place, especially on an animal that can dive down thousands

The New England Aquarium attached this satellite tag to the dorsal fin of a pilot whale that had been rescued from a mass whale stranding, rehabilitated, and released again to the wild. The tag enabled scientists to follow the whale for several months.

of feet. Although Pete Klimley had used a harpoon to place colored streamer tags on sharks in a hammerhead school, he needed a different kind of tag to follow sharks when they disappeared into the depths at night.

Pete decided to use a special device called an ultrasonic telemetry tag, which is a recording device that uses sensors and a small computer chip to record information such as water temperature, depth, and light level and send it to a listening station somewhere in the distance. The computer translates the data into pulses of ultrasonic sound, which are above the human hearing range. In Pete's case, research support vessels floating in the ocean above received the coded messages and translated the information.

While holding his breath, Pete dove into a school of hammerheads with the ultrasonic telemetry tag attached to a dart on the end of a pole. He was able to embed the dart into the muscle between a shark's two dorsal fins. With the dart in place, the slightly buoyant transmitter floated just above the shark, dangling by a thin but powerful monofilament line.

Pete tracked the hammerheads. He discovered that they left the seamount near Espiritu Santo at dusk and went out in very predictable patterns to specific far-away locations.

"When the sun sets, they leave the seamount either in small groups or individually. They travel up to ten miles and stop at a certain time, say 1 A.M. Later in the morning they turn around and generally come back along the same path." Based on what he knew about the hammerhead diet, Pete guessed that they were feeding on squid and fish while they were out on their evening hunt.

"The sensors also transmit information about heading, dive depth, water temperature, and the like," Pete added, "so we can not only

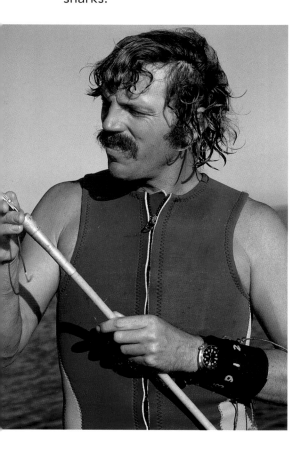

Below: Pete prepares a tag.

Below, right: One of the tags Pete used for hammerhead sharks.

20

Pete uses a pole to attach a tag to a hammerhead shark.

track movement but also learn about behavior and the environment that they're orienting in. The heading sensor has shown that they move with the directionality of a car moving on a highway. Being in the ocean a lot and knowing the great variability in currents, speeds, and directions, I was stunned that the animals could do that."

Scientists are fascinated by the mysteries of animal migration. It makes sense that long-distance migrators like the Arctic tern use the position of the sun during the day and the moon and stars at night to chart a course to feeding grounds thousands of miles away. But what signposts are the hammerhead sharks following in water too deep and too dark for the stars to guide them? Although they swim at depths of over one thousand feet, they can't see the ocean bottom.

Pete tested water currents and water temperature to see if the sharks rely on these cues for underwater navigation. But when he dropped current meters and temperature probes into the shark's nightly migration route, there was no clear pattern.

Pete had one more hunch. Could the sharks use their sensitivity to the earth's magnetic field to navigate? Think of planet Earth as a huge sphere with a giant bar magnet running through its center from near the North Pole to the South Pole. This is the magnetic force that attracts the metallic needle of a compass. It also affects the metals buried in the earth's rocks, whether they are part of a mountain on the land or in an underwater seamount. Pete thought that these invisible force fields might be signposts for the sharks.

From studying the work of a scientist named Adrianus Kalmijn, Pete knew that sharks have an "electromagnetic" sense for which they use thousands of tiny holes or pores on their heads and bodies called the Ampullae of Lorenzini. These tiny pores lead to jelly-filled canals that end in small, vase-shaped sacs (and thus called *ampullae*, which is Greek for

A close-up of the head of a scalloped hammerhead shows the large surface area where thousands of little pores enable the shark to detect magnetic signatures in the rocks around it.

"vase," by their discoverer, Lorenzini). These Ampullae are sensitive to weak electric fields and contain nerve endings that communicate with the shark's brain.

Pete had learned that sharks use the Ampullae of Lorenzini to detect the weak electric currents that all living creatures produce. Young hammerheads, for example, can sense the heartbeat of a fish buried in the sand and chase it out of hiding. This same sense may allow the shark to follow the earth's magnetic field and then use it as a map.

If the hammerheads could detect the magnetic fields encoded in the rocks of their underwater world, that still didn't answer why they returned to the same seamount where they spent their days. To find out more, Pete used a machine called a magnetometer to make a profile of the Espiritu Santo seamount and its surroundings. A magnetometer measures magnetic field strength. One of its uses in the ocean is to locate the iron of sunken ships and buried pipes. Pete dragged his magnetometer behind his boat, using sonar equipment to create an underwater map showing mountains, ridges, and valleys and the magnetic strengths at the various locations.

What Pete found was astounding. The hammerhead sharks he had tagged "seem to orient to minute magnetic patterns of intensity. The sea floor has north-south-directed bands of strong and weak magnetization, which are created during the secretion of ocean crust." Because seamounts such as the one near Espiritu Santo are generally volcanic, they have strong magnetic fields with positive and negative poles, and they stand out from the background magnetic fields, becoming landmarks apart from the rest of the ocean.

Using the seamount as a home base, hammerheads would go out to hunt at night "following less prominent magnetic valleys and ridges that projected outward from the seamount like the spokes of a bicycle wheel." They would then return to the seamount the next morning by following these same magnetic road signs.

Pete also discovered that the peculiar shape and size of the hammerhead shark's head helps it to navigate the underwater highways. "The head spreads the sensors apart, so if there is a very small intensity increase, the left side of the head receives a different reading from the right side. It serves in a sense as what geophysicists call a gradiometer, a detector of a difference in intensity. This would give the animals an ability to remain at one site during the day, then go back to a specific site at night to feed."

Pete Klimley stayed in Boston only for a day, but he continued to share with me his knowledge of the sharks and his ideas for the IMAX film through e-mail and telephone calls. I was energized by his visit, ready to meet the sharks on location. I knew that many of Pete's theories about hammerhead navigation are just that: theories that new research will confirm, refine, or even turn upside-down. But that's what makes science so exciting. That's what keeps scientists like Pete Klimley searching for the questions and answers to help us understand life on our planet. That's what filled me with anticipation as I packed my diving gear for Cocos Island.

Like underwater seamounts, volcanic outcrops such as these can produce strong magnetic fields.

Island of the Sharks

In July 1998, more than six months after Pete Klimley and I had met at the aquarium, I was on an airplane out of Boston heading for Costa Rica. Two thousand miles south of the Baja Peninsula, where Pete Klimley had discovered schools of hammerhead sharks, lies a tiny island called Cocos, which is 330 miles off the Pacific coast of Costa Rica. Espiritu Santo, Cocos, and a group of islands called the Galápagos, which are 350 miles south of Cocos, share a similar geological history. They were formed by volcanoes, and they are a small part of a geologically turbulent area around the Pacific Ocean called the Ring of Fire. Because of the frequent volcanic eruptions and earthquakes, the underwater landscape is filled with seamounts of the kind that Pete Klimley found off Baja.

It was midsummer, and the IMAX camera crew was nearing the end of an entire year of filming. Howard Hall, one of the world's finest underwater cinematographers, was the film's director as well as the main camera operator. His wife, Michele, was the film's producer, and she complemented Howard's camera work with still photography. The Halls had assembled an impressive team of divers, technicians, and photographers to help capture the "island of the sharks" on film. They had already recorded amazing footage of never-seen-before underwater life. But the lingering effects of the weather pattern known as El Niño were keeping the hammerhead sharks away from the seamount.

Pete Klimley had noticed that hammerheads avoided Baja during El Niño

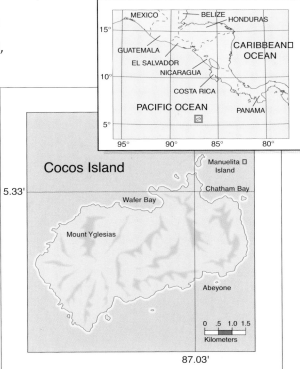

Above: Graffiti on rocks at Chatham Bay records visits by early sailors. Cocos Island is said to have inspired the book *Treasure Island.*

Below: The lush vegetation of Cocos Island.

COCOS ISLAND

Cocos Island is 330 miles from the town of Puntarenas on the Pacific coast of Costa Rica. Five degrees north of the equator, Cocos is only 7.2 miles (12 kilometers) long and 3 miles (5 kilometers) wide.

The island supports a tropical rain forest that receives up to twenty-five feet of rain a year. It shelters three unique species of birds—the Cocos Island flycatcher, cuckoo, and finch—and two endemic reptiles, the anolis lizard and a species of gecko. Red-footed and brown boobies, white terns called fairy terns, and frigate birds make nests on adjacent small islands and rocks.

Largely untouched for most of its history, except for visits by pirates and fishermen, Cocos remains uninhabited today, with the exception of the ranger stations in its two protected harbors, Chatham Bay and Wafer Bay.

Cocos Island formed as the result of volcanic eruptions millions of years ago. Its isolation, upwelling of nutrients, and fringing reefs have created an environment that supports large populations of open-ocean migrators such as billfishes, tuna, manta rays, and sharks, as well as an abundant permanent population of reef fishes and invertebrates. Some fishes take advantage of eddies that flow past the seamounts to seasonally release their eggs. Here the developing young remain trapped in circling currents until they are ready to settle and return to the reefs.

years. They were also avoiding the waters off Costa Rica, and since the hammerheads were the stars of the film, their scarcity around Cocos was a problem.

After my plane landed in San José, Costa Rica's capital city, I boarded a bus for the sleepy fishing port of Puntarenas and then got a ride on the *Okeanos,* one of two expediton boats that have permits to visit Cocos Island. The *Okeanos,* a 120-foot-long dive boat, is equipped with everything a scuba diver could want and more: a virtually unlimited supply of compressed air to fill scuba tanks, a huge dining room, sleeping cabins for fifteen, and even a video player to watch the movies made on the latest dive.

By the time I had unloaded my gear and settled into my assigned cabin, the sun had begun to set. It filled the harbor with a rose and purple glow, which only added to my mounting sense of adventure. I spent the hours of the ocean voyage meeting new companions from Britain, America, and Costa Rica, sharing stories of previous dive expeditions, and thinking about sharks.

Thirty-six hours after we left Puntarenas, the muffled sound of the *Okeanos's* anchor chain announced our arrival in a small protected harbor called Chatham Bay. Our long passage was marked only by the gentle, rolling swells of the ocean. It was four o'clock in the morning, and I decided to remain in my bunk until morning light. I thought about Pete Klimley and how it had taken him more than a year of searching before he saw his first

Top: The *Okeanos* took me to Cocos.

Bottom: Puntarenas harbor.

The *Undersea Hunter* was home base for the IMAX team making the movie *Island of the Sharks*.

hammerhead shark. Here I was, thousands of miles from home and hundreds of miles from land, and I had only ten days.

When I came out on deck a little after 6:00 A.M., the only other boat in the harbor was the *Undersea Hunter,* carrying the IMAX crew. It was already on the move to find the morning's best filming opportunity. What a sight to see the huge cliffs of the nearby island rise out of sight into a blanket of scattered clouds! Unlike the mostly desertlike Baja and the island of Espiritu Santo, Cocos Island is covered with a thick forest of endless green.

I couldn't wait to get into the water, so I decided to explore on my own with the diving guides on the *Okeanos.* The first morning the *Okeanos* stayed anchored while we used rubber boats to reach a diving spot just off a small island called Manuelita a few hundred feet from Cocos Island. Manuelita was stuffed with the nests of brown boobies, foot-tall sea-birds that look as if they are wearing furry brown snowsuits—the kind with drawstrings that pull tight around the face. The birds filled the air with their noisy cackles and constant flight.

Before we put on our scuba gear, our guides used a blackboard to brief us on the dive. They outlined the coral reef and volcanic rocks below, the depth to which we would be diving, the direction we would swim once we reached the bottom, and where we would return to the surface. They also told us the different kinds of fishes we might see, including hammerhead sharks, and where to look for them.

Diving in these waters is not for the faint-hearted or weak-flippered. On entering the water, I was met by what felt like a fierce underwater wind, a strong current that threatened

EL NIÑO

El Niño is a periodic change in the prevailing winds, ocean currents, temperatures, and weather patterns in the Pacific Ocean. These changes are centered on the equator but also extend north and south. No one knows exactly what brings on these changes, which occur approximately every three to five years, but the effects on ocean life and the western and eastern Pacific coastal areas are often dramatic and destructive.

El Niño occurs only in the Pacific Ocean, but because the changes it brings are so global and destructive, scientists are now looking for ways to predict when it will occur. Among the El Niño monitoring devices is a fleet of seventy moored buoys in the Pacific Ocean with sensors to measure the surface wind, relative humidity, air temperature, and water temperature at the surface and as deep as five hundred meters. You can even visit an Internet site at www.pmel.noaa.gov/tao/el-nino/nino-home.html to monitor the daily changes.

No one knows exactly why scalloped hammerheads and other open-ocean travelers seem to avoid areas where the water temperatures reach 80 degrees Fahrenheit or more. One reason may be that higher-than-normal water temperatures and fluctuations in prevailing winds change the composition of the food chain, so that preferred foods are temporarily unavailable.

Coral bleaching results from the loss of algae living in the tissue of coral animals. It is visible around the island because of rising water temperatures, perhaps the result of global climate change.

Above: A nesting redfoot booby.

Right: The dramatic cliffsides of Cocos Island.

Below: A fluffy booby chick.

to sweep me out of sight of my companions. This was a good sign for sighting hammerhead sharks, because the currents bring cold water from the depths. The best I could do was keep going with the current and hope it wouldn't carry me out into deeper ocean waters.

Occasionally I grabbed a clump of large, pinkish "gooseneck" barnacles to stop my momentum and to exchange glances with the small fishes hiding in nearby crevices. During one of these rest periods, out of the corner of my eye, I caught sight of my first hammerhead shark. It looked to be about five feet long and was swimming alone, swinging its head and body slowly back and forth over the coral bottom. Although it came within twenty feet, it showed no interest in me and kept on swimming, lost in its own world. In noting the way it was swinging its head, I recognized the signs Pete Klimley had described of hammerheads searching for food or for the magnetic field locked in the volcanic rocks.

The morning dive at Manuelita was just a warm-up for an afternoon at Dirty Rock. One of the favorite sites for visiting divers, Dirty Rock is a small mountain of jagged rocks that thrusts up out of the water about five hundred feet from Manuelita and the neighboring Cocos. As we slid into the water from our rubber support boat, we followed the wall of rock down one hundred feet to a sandy bottom and waited for our guide, Alberto.

The first part of the dive would take us along the base of Dirty Rock until we reached one end of the island. From there Alberto would lead us off into the blue, leaving all signposts behind. I realized that I had to do what the hammerhead sharks do much of the time, navigate without any visual landmarks. Whereas hammerheads have the possible

Above: These rubber boats take divers to the location of the day's dive.

Below: Small fishes shelter in the coral reef.

The hieroglyph fish.

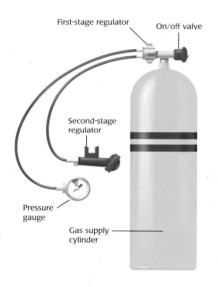

First-stage regulator

On/off valve

Second-stage regulator

Pressure gauge

Gas supply cylinder

SCUBA (Self Contained Underwater Breathing Apparatus)

Jacques Yves Cousteau and Emil Gagnan invented the Aqualung, now known as the scuba tank, in 1943. The modern "open-circuit" scuba tank contains air compressed from the air around us. It is called "open-circuit" because the diver releases the exhaled gases into the surrounding water. The gases in a conventional scuba tank are a mixture of 21 percent oxygen and 78 percent nitrogen, as well as a few trace gases, all squeezed into a sturdy steel or aluminum bottle a few feet long.

The gases are compressed to provide an efficient source of air and to deliver it at pressure to counteract the weight of water on divers' bodies, which increases as they go deeper. Divers use a regulator with a mouthpiece to breathe compressed air in an amount and at a pressure that is safe for their lungs. They exhale the unused oxygen, nitrogen, and carbon dioxide as bubbles released through side vents in their regulator. With each inhale and exhale, the body absorbs the oxygen and nitrogen it needs and gets rid of potentially dangerous metabolic waste products in the form of carbon dioxide.

advantage of "seeing" with a magnetic sense, I had just my eyes. Our destination was a series of small underwater peaks. There we hoped to see sharks coming in from the deep.

My diving companions included a retired Japanese businessman named Oak-san. He was a small man of over seventy years, with a twinkle in his eye and an adventuresome spirit, and the yellow gloves he wore served as a beacon to me as our group of seven divers swam single file out into stark blue waters, with no land in sight. Because it was an overcast day, the bubbles rising from our scuba tanks were the only way we knew where the surface was. Suddenly, out of nowhere, another single line of swimmers appeared twenty feet below us: they were hammerhead sharks. Humans and sharks were swimming toward the same destination.

Pete Klimley had never talked about hammerhead cleaning stations in the Gulf of California (although he later told me that they definitely exist there). They were one of the big discoveries for me off Cocos Island, and they gave me a new appreciation for one of the reasons hammerhead sharks gather around seamounts. A cleaning station is a little like an underwater barbershop except that fish don't get haircuts there. Instead, fish with parasites on their skin and in their gills and mouths stop in to seek out other specialist fish called cleaner fish. The cleaner fish get a meal as they remove the parasites from the others. Below me, the single line of hammerhead sharks was making its way to a nearby cleaning station, where small striped fish called barberfish were ready to offer their services.

As my diving companions and I reached our destination—a pinnacle that rose from the deep—we each found a convenient place to stand and watch. By now, the small line of sharks that we had seen earlier was parading just at the edge of our visibility. One by one, sharks glided closer to the swarm of expectant barberfish. I saw a cleaner fish enter the opening of a shark's gills, picking with its small mouth. It was so successful at getting rid of the gill parasites that I could see the shark respond with an appreciative shudder.

Oak-san aboard the *Okeanos* dive boat.

Hammerheads Close Up

My first glimpse of a small school of hammerhead sharks whetted my appetite for more. Pete Klimley had described hammerheads schooling in the hundreds, even thousands, and that was, after all, what the IMAX crew had come to see. Until I got lucky, I decided to watch filmmakers Howard and Michele Hall put some of the final touches on their film.

Since the film team still had one more trip to Cocos scheduled a few months later, they could use the time to fill in gaps in a story line that included whitetip and blacktip sharks, sea turtles, marble rays, sea stars, and a host of other small invertebrates. If the hammerheads returned in the hoped-for large numbers sometime on this trip, so much the better. In the meantime, Howard wanted to dramatize the cold-water currents as they flowed through the warmer surrounding water like icy streams.

Upwelling occurs when ocean currents encounter Cocos Island and its adjacent seamounts. Cold, nutrient-rich waters are forced to the surface, where they energize a food chain that begins with tiny floating plants and animals called plankton. As the plankton flourish, they support clams, snails, shrimp, worms, and other small creatures that are eaten by larger animals, such as stingrays and groupers, which in turn are eaten by sharks.

Sharks, billfish, tuna, and other large predatory fishes play a vital role in the ocean ecosystem. These "apex predators" are at the top of the food web, with few natural predators. They feed on sick or weak animals and keep populations under control. They also help control disease, maintain species diversity, and allow the fittest animals to reproduce.

Opposite: Hammerheads around Cocos Island come inshore to find parasite feeding cleaners like the butterfly fish.

Below: Howard and Michele Hall were the directors, producers, and camera operators of the IMAX film.

Howard doesn't use a scuba tank to breathe underwater, because the exhaled air produces too many bubbles that frighten the fish he wants to film. For scientists and film-makers, a system called a closed-circuit rebreather is often the equipment of choice. It enables the same kind of close observations that Pete Klimley had made in free diving off Baja before rebreathing technology had become available.

Among the advantages to the closed-circuit rebreather is the way it "scrubs" or absorbs the carbon dioxide exhaled in every breath. If too much carbon dioxide accumulates in the lungs, it can become deadly. The carbon dioxide scrubber allows divers to rebreathe their exhaled breath by removing most of the dangerous carbon dioxide.

The rebreather also reduces the nitrogen inhaled. As a diver surfaces, it's imperative that he or she limit the amount of nitrogen accumulated in the body during a dive and the amount that remains upon surfacing. If the diver fails to do this, the nitrogen forms large bubbles in the bloodstream, which can block the flow of oxygen to the heart or collect in the joints (also known as decompression sickness). By replacing some of the nitrogen in the breathing mixture with more oxygen or a gas such as helium, divers can spend more time underwater safely.

On the second to last day of my visit, I got the opportunity I had been waiting for. The skies were clear and sunny early in the day, and Howard decided to explore a seamount called Alcyone, because it was one of the best places to see schools of hammerhead sharks. At first I couldn't dive with the rest of the team because I was not trained in how to use the rebreather, and bubbles from a scuba tank might frighten away the fish.

By midmorning the skies had turned a dull and muddy gray and blasts of wind and rain showers covered the horizon. Bouncing around on a boat in the choppy ocean was making

Sometimes it takes two divers to stabilize the IMAX camera and take it from one underwater site to another.

REBREATHERS

Filmmaker Howard Hall uses a system called a closed-circuit rebreather. Every breath he exhales is recycled by the breathing apparatus on his back. No bubbles of air escape to the surrounding water (a semiclosed system releases a little bit of air).

Howard's closed-circuit rebreather has four main components contained in a backpack weighing eighty pounds: two steel spheres nine inches in diameter, one of which contains pure oxygen and the other a mixture of gases such as nitrogen, oxygen, and helium; a carbon dioxide "scrubber" that looks like the air filter in an automobile; and a "counterlung," a flexible structure like the pouch of a bagpipe, which takes in and empties gases on their way back to the diver.

A closed-circuit rebreather is a complex system of sensors and gas delivery units that Howard and his technicians monitor carefully, constantly cleaning and replacing parts. Because of the danger involved, he has designed a bailout feature to the system so he can breathe the regular compressed air of a scuba tank if the rebreather malfunctions.

Howard Hall displays the closed-circuit rebreather that he uses while filming. It is a variation of the model shown below.

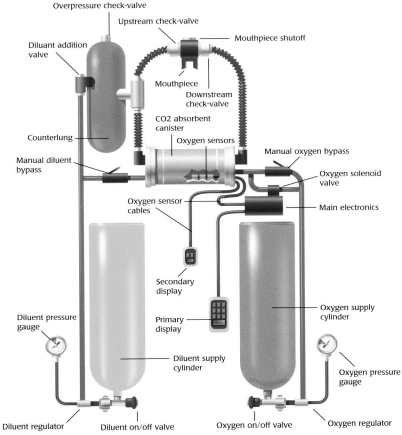

Overpressure check-valve

Upstream check-valve

Mouthpiece shutoff

Diluant addition valve

Mouthpiece

Downstream check-valve

CO_2 absorbent canister

Counterlung

Oxygen sensors

Manual oxygen bypass

Manual diluent bypass

Oxygen solenoid valve

Oxygen sensor cables

Main electronics

Secondary display

Diluent pressure gauge

Primary display

Oxygen supply cylinder

Diluent supply cylinder

Oxygen pressure gauge

Diluent regulator

Diluent on/off valve

Oxygen on/off valve

Oxygen regulator

me feel seasick, so Howard's voice over the intercom brought welcome relief. It was OK for me to come down now, since he had all the IMAX shots he needed for the moment. With my eyes fixed on the underwater plateau ninety feet below, I entered the water and worked my way to the nearest outcropping of coral rock, where Howard had set up the tripod he needed to stabilize the IMAX camera. The camera itself weighs 250 pounds out of water, and although most of that weight is buoyant underwater, it has a will of its own in stiff underwater currents.

At first I could see only my diving companions among the rocks, because the morning storm and heavy currents made for poor visibility. But even the gray, dimly lit water didn't stop me from seeing what happened next. Like a flock of birds covering the sky, forty to fifty hammerhead sharks glided lazily above us from north to south, blocking my view of the surface. And that was just the beginning. One after another, new schools entered from different directions. In an awesome display of coordinated movement, they floated like clouds above us for five to ten minutes. Then, as quickly as they had appeared, the hammerheads were gone.

The sharks' sudden disappearance left me and my diving companions with a feeling of privilege and loss: privilege at witnessing this moving display of some of the ocean's most enduring and evocative creatures, and loss at the sense that gatherings such as these may be disappearing from the face of the planet.

Above: The IMAX team poses with the 250-pound IMAX camera before it is lowered into the ocean by a crane.

Below: IMAX filming of sea stars.

Postscript

Howard Hall took close-up photos of hammerheads that day in early August, but he had to wait until October to capture the best images for the film's final cut. I left the film crew with visions of sharks imprinted on my memory and a rare glimpse into the making of an IMAX film. I also realized how well the time I spent with Pete Klimley had served me.

There are still many questions to answer about hammerhead sharks. Pete is working on some of them already. If his theory about shark migration proves to be accurate, it may confirm the importance of seamounts like those around the Baja Peninsula and Cocos Island as stepping stones to navigate the ocean. It may also lead to the safeguarding of sharks and other open-ocean travelers from the uncontrolled fishing that is now decimating their populations.

The United Nations Educational, Scientific, and Cultural Organization (UNESCO) declared Cocos Island a World Heritage Site in 1997, recognizing it as a world resource deserving special protection from fishing and habitat abuse. Fishing is prohibited in a zone up to seven miles off its coast, and it might be hoped that someday the Mexican government will decide to declare the same kind of sanctuary for parts of the Baja Peninsula. One thing is certain: the more we learn about the importance of oases in the ocean, the more we will try to protect the ones we have for the wildlife that depends on them for survival.

Pete's Work Continues

Pete Klimley has a list of unanswered questions about hammerhead sharks, but so far El Niño and possibly global warming seem to be getting in the way. While he waits for the hammerheads to return during their usual visiting times from May to November in the Gulf of California, Pete has been tagging yellowfin tuna and using his listening stations to understand when and where they go. By tagging tuna, billfish, and other seamount visitors, Pete hopes to find out if the fishes that customarily appear with the hammerheads make up a predictable community.

"Do they come and go as a group?" he wonders. "If they don't, what determines when each species comes? We need to be better at predicting when these species come and go, which could be important to fisheries and for the answers to questions such as 'Is the Gulf of California a dying sea?' Last summer, it looked like a dying sea. But knowledge of how abundances of species fluctuate from year to year based on events like El Niño is necessary to answer such questions."

Another unsolved mystery is where the hammerheads go in their yearly migrations. "Where do they go when they leave the seamount for good—not just for the night—as they do every year." Pete wonders. "When do they leave? How far do they go? Do they have a chronological set of way points at which they stop? I suspect that they don't go just anywhere. They go to a specific place at a specific time and then go to the next place at a specific time and then the next place, and they do this together. I'd be very interested to learn more about that."

He would also like to definitively prove that hammerheads indeed detect the seamount

A baitball is a mass of schooling fish that spin helplessly in front of the gathered predators, which rush through their midst, feeding on the defenseless school.

Shark populations are in trouble from overfishing and from useless and wasteful killing in nets intended for other prey.

by the magnetic field. "Years ago I proposed winding a huge wire coil around the Espiritu Santo seamount," Pete says. "The hammerheads are found just on the north side of the mount, not on the south side; this is true, in fact, of the whole pelagic assemblage [all of the open-ocean fishes]. I wanted to know if, by reversing the mount's polarity, the sharks would move to the southern side of the seamount. If they did, it would indicate that the sharks are orienting to a specific part of the seamount based on the positive or negative pull of the magnetic field."

Shark Conservation

Sharks have a reputation for being vicious killers, but humans are much more of a threat to sharks than they are to us. There are between eight and twelve human fatalities a year because of sharks worldwide, while our fishing activities are responsible for the death of between twenty million and one hundred million sharks in the same period of time.

Many sharks are killed just for their fins, which are worth from twenty-five dollars to over one hundred dollars a pound in the United States when sold for shark-fin soup. Growing demand for fins has contributed to a decline in shark populations worldwide. Especially before its designation as a World Heritage Site, Cocos Island had been the site of shark finning for several species, including the hammerhead.

Sharks are also killed by accident. Modern fishing methods use huge nets that catch everything in their path. When the nets accidentally capture sharks, dolphins, sea birds, and turtles, these animals, injured from the nets, are simply tossed back into the sea to die. This needless killing, called "bycatch," claims an estimated 30 million tons of fish, or one fifth of all fish taken from the ocean.

As a group, sharks are in danger of extinction because of their unique life cycle, which is unlike those of most fish. They mature slowly, have a long gestation period, grow slowly, produce few young at one time, and often depend on inshore, coastal nursery areas that are threatened by human development and recreation.

Sunset shows Manuelita Island in all its splendor.

What Can You Do to Help Sharks?

- Do not purchase any products containing shark parts, including shark-fin soup, shark skin, or shark liver oil.

- Don't buy shark steaks, shark jaws, or shark teeth.

- There is little or no support for the effectiveness of shark cartilage in fighting disease when taken as a food supplement: don't buy shark cartilage for yourself or your pets.

- Educate everyone you know about the importance of sharks in the ocean and the importance of coral reefs in supporting ocean wildlife.

- Support local and global legislation for the protection of sharks.

- When diving, give sharks the space they need: respect wildlife.

- If you dive or snorkel near coral reefs, don't touch, stand on, or collect coral, and respect regulations about capturing, feeding, and handling marine life.

- Practice catch and release if you fish for sharks for sport. Take home photos instead.

The IMAX film crew used a custom-built ultralight to film dramatic aerials of the island.

Suggestions for Further Reading

BOOKS

Banister, Keith. *A Look Inside Sharks and Rays.* Westport, Conn.: Joshua Morris Publishing, 1995.

Cerullo, Mary M. *The Little Guides: Sharks.* Ed. Leighton Taylor. San Francisco: Weldon Owen, 1999.

———. *The Truth About Great White Sharks.* San Francisco: Chronicle Books, 2000.

Markle, Sandra. *Outside and Inside Sharks.* New York: Simon & Schuster, 1996.

Maynard, Christopher. *Informania Sharks.* Cambridge, Mass.: Candlewick Press, 1997.

McGovern, Ann. *Shark Lady: True Adventures of Eugenie Clark.* Illus. Ruth Chew. New York: Scholastic, 1998.

Springer, Victor, and Joy P. Gold. *Sharks in Question: The Smithsonian Answer Book.* Washington, D.C.: Smithsonian Institution Press, 1989.

Stevens, John D., ed. *Sharks.* 2d edition. New York: Facts on File Publications, 1999.

WEB SITE RESOURCES

The Cocos Island Research Center: **www.istmo.com/cocos**

At this quirky, enjoyable site, delve into the island's unique history, including its recent designation as a UNESCO World Heritage Site, and explore scads of useful links.

IUCN Shark Specialist Group: **www.flmnh.ufl.edu/fish/Organizations/SSG**

Learn how the Shark Specialist Group is working to help conserve threatened species of sharks worldwide.

Mote Marine Laboratory: The Center for Shark Research: **www.motemarine.org/~rhueter/sharks**

This nonprofit institution's site offers information on shark diversity, tagging, and attacks, as well as descriptions of their research programs on shark vision, feeding, and more.

New England Aquarium: **www.neaq.org**

This is the Web site of the New England Aquarium, cosponsor with WGBH of *Island of the Sharks.*

NOVA Online WGBH/NOVA: **www.pbs.org/wgbh/nova**

NOVA Online gives an imaginative and in-depth view of the making of the IMAX film *Island of the Sharks.*

The Pelagic Shark Research Foundation: **www.pelagic.org**

This foundation works to develop projects that contribute to a better understanding of sharks. Check out the shark video clips, find out about the sharks of Monterey Bay, and read about shark evolution and anatomy.

The *Undersea Hunter:* **www.underseahunter.com**

This thorough site gives you everything you'd ever want to know about the *Undersea Hunter,* the live-aboard dive boat on which this expedition is based at Cocos Island.

Nests of brown boobies cover Manuelita Island.

Index